WHY DO BEARS HIBERNATE?

Animal Book Grade 2
Children's Animal Books

BABY PROFESSOR
EDUCATION KIDS

Speedy Publishing LLC
40 E. Main St. #1156
Newark, DE 19711
www.speedypublishing.com

In this book, we're going to talk about why bears hibernate. So, let's get right to it!

Imagine that you are out in the forest. It's the wintertime, and you are cold and hungry. There's nothing to eat so you make a den underground, fill it with straw to lie down on, and then you go to sleep. However, this sleep isn't like your regular sleep. Maybe you go into hibernation for three or four months or longer. You might not eat or go to the bathroom that whole time.

Polar Bear

When you wake up, go back to your house, and get on the bathroom scale you might weigh ten pounds less than you did before you hibernated. Now you know a little about what it means when animals hibernate. Even though there have been a few extreme cases where people's bodies went into a state of hibernation, for the most part people don't hibernate.

WHAT IS HIBERNATION?

Hibernation is a process that many animals use to save energy. It's used to survive the intensely cold winter without having to migrate to somewhere warmer. Some animals in very hot climates go through a form of hibernation called aestivation. It works similarly to hibernation and allows them to survive the heat.

Black Bear

Hibernating is like sleeping, but it's more intense. Depending on which species is doing the hibernating, an animal might just have brief times where it isn't active. On the hand, some species go so deeply asleep that they are unconscious for long periods of time.

Hibernation can be risky because an animal in this dormant condition can be attacked by predators.

Hibernating Bats

WHICH TYPES OF ANIMALS HIBERNATE?

Lots of small mammals hibernate during the winter. Chipmunks, hedgehogs, and bats all hibernate. Many types of insects, as well as reptiles and amphibians hibernate too.

HOW DOES HIBERNATION WORK?

When an animal hibernates, its metabolism slows down and its internal temperature decreases. For example, the temperature of a ground squirrel is usually 99 degrees Fahrenheit, but during hibernation it goes down to 27 degrees Fahrenheit. The animal's breathing and heart rate slows down too.

Ground Squirrel

Brown Bat

For example, a bat's heartbeat is usually about 400 times in a minute, but when it hibernates its heartbeat goes down to about 11 beats a minute. There are even some animals that have special antifreeze in their blood so they can freeze solid and survive when they thaw out. Wood frogs freeze during the winter and thaw out when the temperature warms up.

WHAT IS KNOWN ABOUT WHETHER BEARS HIBERNATE?

Until just recently, scientists weren't too sure about whether bears hibernated or not. They were pretty sure that they did since they disappeared into their dens for months. They came out in the spring looking much skinnier than they went in. However, there was a problem with doing scientific research to discover more.

Polar Bear

There are plenty of bears in zoos but they don't behave the same way that bears in the wild do, so that wouldn't work for true scientific study. After all, who wants to run the risk of going into a den where a wild, sleeping bear might wake up?

With smaller mammals, such as ground squirrels or bats, scientists have been able to study them in the laboratory or wire them up in their native habitats. This is how they found out that when they hibernate they're just 2% different from being dead.

Hibernating Bat

Grizzly Bear

However, what they found out about small animals didn't necessarily apply to big animals like bears. They knew that the only way to find out about bears was to set up an experiment in the wild to see what bears really do.

AN EXPERIMENT WITH BLACK BEARS

A group of scientists persuaded some state wildlife officers to let them have several black bears that had been captured in Alaska. The animals were brought to the Arctic Biology Institute. There, the scientists put some sensors inside the bears so they could monitor their biology, like their heartbeats.

Black Bear

American Black Bears

Then, they brought the bears to a safe wooded area. In the woods they had built special dens for the black bears. These manmade dens had the straw from the bears' own dens fluffed up with some new fresh straw that the scientists had added.

As winter approached, the bears got ready for their extended sleep. Meanwhile, the scientists were watching them. As the scientists thought they would, the bears curled up in the straw and slept. They changed their positions just one or two times every day. Sometimes they stood up or groomed themselves just a little, then they moved their straw around, just like you might move your blankets or your pillow, before they went back down to sleep.

Baby Black Bear In Snow

The most important thing that the scientists were able to get information about was the bears' internal temperature. Human beings have an internal temperature of about 98 degrees Fahrenheit.

Bears have an internal temperature around 100.4 degrees Fahrenheit. When they slept, their temperature went down to 85 degrees Fahrenheit. This was a sizable drop, but not as much of a drop as the true hibernators like ground squirrels.

Their heart rates varied a great deal and depended on what state of sleep they were in. Sometimes if they got too cold, they would begin to shiver and their heart rates would go up.

As far as their metabolism rates, they dropped down to 25% of normal, not like the true hibernators whose metabolism dropped down to only 2% of their normal metabolism. When the bears came out of their winter slumber, it was weeks before they were feeling at full strength again. Just imagine how you would feel if you slept from Christmas Day until Valentine's Day. You'd be groggy too!

Their conclusion was that bears are "light" hibernators. Their bodies need a lot more energy to function so they can't hibernate in the same way as other animals do. They are alert to danger and will wake up if anything in their environment could be putting them at risk. During these winter hibernating months, pregnant female bears give birth to their cubs so they have to be alert to protect their cubs.

HOW DO BEARS AVOID POOPING FOR SO LONG?

The bears shed cells from their bodies even though they aren't eating during the winter months. They also groom themselves. This waste matter forms a dry "plug" at the end of their intestines so they don't poop during hibernation. When they come out of their dens, they poop out this plug and their digestion goes back to its normal process.

WHY WAS THIS EXPERIMENT IMPORTANT?

The science of how bears hibernate might help human beings someday. The findings might point the way to new medical therapies. For example, if someone was very ill, the doctor might be able to put that person into a state of hibernation until a cure was found. Another application might be for someone who is waiting for an organ transplant.

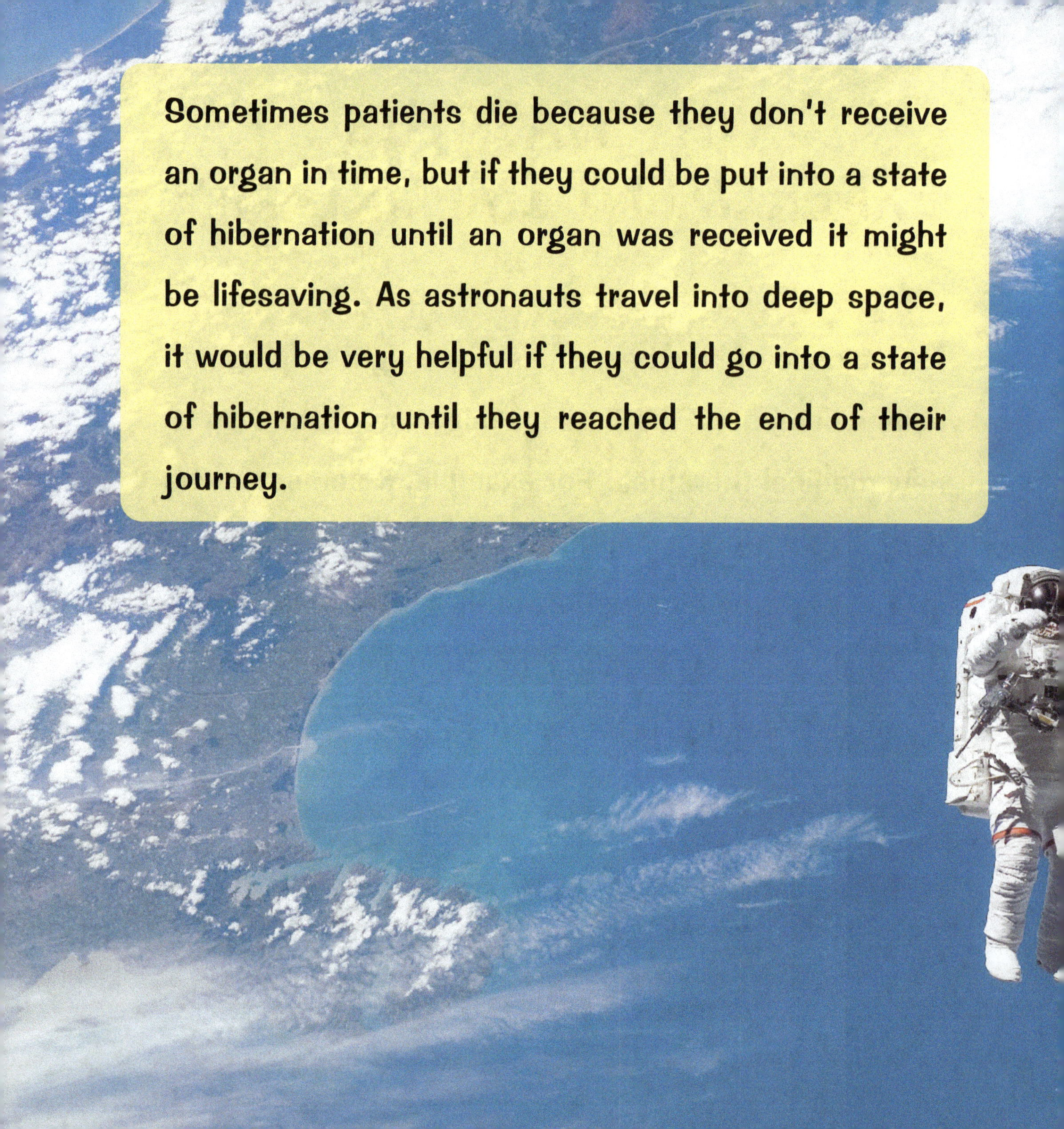

Sometimes patients die because they don't receive an organ in time, but if they could be put into a state of hibernation until an organ was received it might be lifesaving. As astronauts travel into deep space, it would be very helpful if they could go into a state of hibernation until they reached the end of their journey.

Polar Bear and Cubs

WHY DO BEARS HIBERNATE?

Bears hibernate to survive the winter cold. What the scientists found out is that bears don't truly hibernate the same way other smaller mammals do. They do this to save their energy so they can survive during the intense cold. They spend most of the winter days asleep deep inside their dens. Their metabolism and heart rates slow down, but they don't decrease as much as small mammals that are true hibernators.

A bear that is in "light" hibernation can go for over 3 months without pooping, peeing, drinking water, or eating any food. True hibernators, such as chipmunks, have to wake up on a regular basis to eliminate waste and eat stored food before going back to their dormant state.

The other difference is that true hibernators aren't easy to awaken. Bears can be easily awakened from their sleep. Another reason not to go into a cave with a bear that's in light hibernation!

Before they go into their dens or caves during the winter, bears eat a lot and store up fat so that they can survive on their fat during the winter. Their cells keep them hydrated and fed since they don't drink or eat during that time. When they come out in the spring, they're really hungry.

Polar Bear

SUMMARY

Bears hibernate so they can survive the harsh winter cold, but they aren't true hibernators like chipmunks, squirrels, hedgehogs, and other small mammals. They do go into a state of "light" hibernation. Unlike true hibernators, they can be easily awakened. True hibernators are hard to wake up. They don't eat, drink, poop, or pee while they are in their caves or dens during their winter sleep. True hibernators wake up on a regular basis so they can eat, drink, and eliminate wastes.

Now that you've learned about the hibernation of bears, you may want to read about some other interesting animals in the Baby Professor book Is It An Alligator or A Crocodile? Animal Book 6 Year Old.

Visit
BABY PROFESSOR
EDUCATION KIDS
www.BabyProfessorBooks.com
to download Free Baby Professor eBooks
and view our catalog of new and exciting
Children's Books

www.ingramcontent.com/pod-product-compliance
Lightning Source LLC
LaVergne TN
LVHW060829170826
845678LV00010B/1932

9798869434784